Wow

Bill Manhire

CARCANET

ACKNOWLEDGEMENTS

Grateful thanks to the editors of nzpoetryshelf.com, *PN Review*, *Poetry*, *Shenandoah*, *Sport*, the *School Journal* and *Turbine | Kapohau*, where a number of these poems first appeared.

First published in Great Britain in 2020 by
Carcanet
Alliance House, 30 Cross Street
Manchester M2 7AQ
www.carcanet.co.uk

Text copyright © Bill Manhire 2020

The right of Bill Manhire to be identified as the author of this work has been asserted in accordance with the Copyright, Designs and Patents Act of 1988; all rights reserved.

A CIP catalogue record for this book is available from the British Library.

ISBN 978 1 80017 004 9

Printed in Great Britain by SRP Ltd, Exeter, Devon

The publisher acknowledges financial assistance from Arts Council England.

For my long-haul editors, Fergus Barrowman and Michael Schmidt

Contents

1

Huia	13
Untitled	14
Also	15
The Armchair Traveller	16
South	17
Side Trips	18
Names	19
A Really Nice Trip	20
Letter from the New Place	21
Sorrow	23
Woodwork	24
Someone Was Burning the Forest	25
Warm Ocean	26
Falling Asleep	32
The Terrible Singers	33

2

Noah	37
Angels	38
The Angry God	39
He Loved Her Lemonade Scones	40
Breakfast	41
The Mysterious Twin	42
The Kaffir Lime Is Having a Bad Day	43
Isolation Notes	44
Mean Neptune	46

To Be Concluded	47
Earthquake Practice	48
Conference Dinner	49
Lives of the Poets	50
Langholm	51
The Lazy Poet	52
The Deerculler's Wife	54
What I'm picking up when I'm out and about	55
Weather	57

3

Discontinued Product	61
After Lockdown	67
Incidental	68
Halls	69
Exhibition	70
The Sailor	72
Knots	74
Our Teacher	75
The Sky	76
Change Nothing	77
Like	78
The Smile	79
Wow	80
Polly	82
Reverse Ovid	83
After Surgery	84

Little Prayers	87

they've cleared away
the clearings

1

Huia

I was the first of birds to sing
I sang to signal rain
the one I loved was singing
and singing once again

My wings were made of sunlight
my tail was made of frost
my song was now a warning
and now a song of love

I sang upon a postage stamp
I sang upon your coins
but money courted beauty
you could not see the joins

Where are you when you vanish?
Where are you when you're found?
I'm made of greed and anguish
a feather on the ground

+

I lived among you once
and now I can't be found
I'm made of things that vanish
a feather on the ground

Untitled

This book about extinct birds is heavier than any bird:
heavier than the dark bird eating my heart,
page after page of abandoned wings.
I lift it up and sit it on my lap
and listen to it purring.

Also

my mother cries all day
because soon it will be the world's last day

imagine being a baby again!
I can't do that but I must try

+

also: my dog's bark
is the whole of the colour blue

it is ice rising out of the sea
and all because he is pleased to see me

The Armchair Traveller

Excuse me if I laugh.
The roads are dark and large books block our path.
The air we breathe is made of evening air.
The world is longer than the road that brings us here.

The necklace is a carving, not a kiss.
You run towards the one you can't resist.
At first she edges backwards, then she stalls.
Now every sentence needs another clause.

The road goes off through willows, then it winds.
Is that the famous temple over there?
Why are the people round about so undefined?
Why must they kiss then disappear?

Time now to let the story take its course,
just settle back and let the driver drive.
Bliss is it late at night to be alive,
learning to yield, and not to strive.

South

There it goes again, the heart,
wayward and lost on the streets
of K——, a city I'll never visit;

and there it was maybe 50 years ago
on some intergalactic mission
a thousand years in the future;

or back here just this morning
in the cold impossible cold,
falling into step beside Shackleton,

whose body beats on through the cold
for as always it is filled
with boats and birds.

Side Trips

1.

We travelled to the town of K——
where all the citizens insist on weeping.
No one who visits there can offer comfort.
You see, the schoolbus departed many years ago,
now there are only parents.

2.

I like the cloud at the top of Shingle Road,
the way it makes my feelings settle.
Sheep can still find grass there,
grazing among a thousand stones.
Each stone was once the shadow of a bird.

3.

God lend you strength, says the too eventful day,
soon you will be home among your loved ones,
soon you will know the beauty of the earth.

Names

Yes, the waterfall is beautiful.
In days gone by this place was called
Where Jennifer Ate Her Final Meal and Afterwards She Slept.
These days we call it Jingle Bells because, well, you know,
our parents always liked that song.

A Really Nice Trip

We went up Pleasant Valley.
After which we came back down to Pleasant Flat.
Then we went all the way out to Pleasant Point.
It was a really nice trip.

Letter from the New Place

I sleep in a house that is not my house,
not my roof, not my rafters,
here at the far end
of the twisting tail of a land
where only a bucket of gravel will break my fall.

All morning filling out forms
half listening to the sea that storms
and stamps and stammers
learning to pick grapes and apples
learning to read a hundred useless things –
I want to see that, I want to see this –
all the problems, all the damage.

Did you hear what happened to
our path of corrugated iron across the mud –
blown away I'm sorry,
blown away alas,
once it was your mother's roof.

Now I walk the long way round
to see the man who says
Are you happy
Are you happy with your house
Are you pregnant once again?

Old words, new words,
a few moments of understanding,
and always quickly lost.

You belong to the new place
and I belong to the new place
where I believe we will one day miss each other.

Also the old place,
also the old place too –
the sails and the almost sand and water,
all the terrifying winds.

Sorrow

I walk around a lot.
I apologise to all and sundry.
I look for pleasure in my mind.

Away with sorrow!
I write this on a page.
I call it out to passers-by.

Repeat a thought a thousand times
and it will live forever.

The god stands behind me
and coughs politely.
You never see him
but he makes himself known.

He says sad is sometimes beautiful.
He says he has a plan for me.

He asks me to imagine
the brain of a dying child.

So hard!

He says I should learn to weep more often.
He thinks this would be helpful.
Each day I am his precious one.

Woodwork

Children are building their teacher a coffin.
There it is in the paper, somewhere in Holland,

a good plain coffin made of many parts,
and two of the children

call each day and talk to the teacher
to keep the teacher posted. Is she happy?

She is ill but quite contented.
What will they give her to take with her

into the earth at last, or across those borders
where only teachers travel? There is dark energy there

and multiplication tables, and many children are in a room
with chisels and planes and spirit levels.

They must be making something wonderful.
Everything needs to be straight.

I made a boat, a tie-rack, a wooden spoon.
The boat sat on a mantelpiece in several different houses.

It was happy with its yellow funnel,
somewhere it is sailing. And everywhere children

are waving and working hard.
They are building their teacher a coffin.

Someone Was Burning the Forest

We did not know why the child was crying,
nor why he stood bare-shouldered at the window.
How had he come by those skimpy feathers?
The mother had fallen from the tower
a moment after she began to answer. I looked around
and there were many towers, also other bodies.
Now I was on the ground myself. I could hear
the child but no longer see him. Perhaps
he was still aloft. The towers were dissolving
yet surely there were trees. It was dark now
but I knew there must be many bodies.
I would need to climb to see where we might go.

Warm Ocean

Someone says lonely let's go for a stroll
someone says not now
someone says it was never about the money
someone says what then
someone says a few basic rules
anger desire compassion
anger desire compassion
and then there's a great silence
in which we all go for a stroll
clifftop ocean a few swimmers far below

+

Old women are swimming in the ocean
there's classical music going on
so many heads bobbing and nodding
where is my lover, where is my lover
the women cry, bobbing and nodding
and they all take up the cry
and violins you know
where is my lover, where is my lover
and now the small girl is asleep

+

Three old men late afternoon
last ones left in the water
come on admiral! says one
but it's not clear which one

or who to – maybe us?
they want us to watch them don't they   no
they want us to go away   no
they want us to set a net
and spend our last days hauling in

+

Long bench where men sat once
stubborn wood
old driftwood trunk
before the vows and boasts
before the oars demanding water
before the killings
before the killings and the weepings
before the poet's song
before the later tales about the killings
the ones they made from fish and cigarettes

+

Long stretch of wood with nothing there
except you know patches of drifting grain
maybe a piece of cloud maybe a tiny stream
a few books
and on the stream-bed the stones knocking together
you can hear them *clock*
when you turn off the noise of the world
there they are going *clock cluck*
clock cluck clock like time itself
a busy creature deep below the surface
each time you put your ear to the timber

+

Well anyway I think I prefer the inland forest
birds with their dings and dongs and dusky wings
making some beauty
making all of us shiver
even when crying there's a sail a sail
telling us over and over yes and forever
that the ghost can't stand the graveyard

+

Ancient man clad in bells
he jumps and terrifies the children
the adults too clang clang
we wonder a bit why we came here
something on the radio perhaps
or maybe the kids had heard it somewhere
anyway here we are yelling at him you fucking
fucking cunt we yell and why
have you come here clanger-cunt! as he runs
into the forest same old forest
followed by all our women
chirping and cheeping and chasing
off once again to hide among the birds

+

The where-am-I bird is singing again
deep in the woods the bush the forest
people lost in the undergrowth
swearing at each other as you do

as you mostly don't when you're hunting
and now the where-am-I bird
is reshining its song
up-in-the-sky up-in-the-sky
everyone looking up high now of course
taking aim and lost for an answer
gone-now-for-good
and now just to settle everything down
the bagarup bird is squawking again
on the general's desk by the caged canary
by the potted daisy oh there's the telephone

+

The god rises up out of the river
so we make the temple on the riverbank
big white flowers like plates we might eat from
then the bodies the blindfolds the blur
and rain puzzled by its own prosperity
one and two and three and others
blessing the coming and the going
the generous bodies hauled high
as blood weeps out of eyes and ankles
the shame and plaque and tangle
so the world will be better now god help us
now that the god is finally helping

+

The huge man carries his tiny candle
he stumbles forward picking people up
then yes tossing them aside

his hand is huge, all handle
he gasps behind his tongue behind his smile
walks into the water *apparently*
and soon he is remote like a ripple
like something sighing
like the troubled echo of a sigh
and someone comes up to us and says
really to anyone who'll listen
how could he come along and leave like that
not even buying a ticket

+

Like possible footprints on the ocean floor
possibly there possibly not
that's the way her memory paces
to and fro to and fro
and who exactly are you anyway
to and fro with your talk of a kiss gone missing
and your all in all and your wherewithal
and all of those things that aren't material
that's not what we want from an answer
no we never wanted anything like that
maybe snow melting and frost in a field
maybe sand that shuffles aside when she whispers

+

Don't play the music don't play the music
says the man
who walks around town saying
over and over don't play the music

all songs being made
as we know from things that hurt
ice that melts flames that fall from the sky
yes all of that and more
all of that and more
and the father goes on singing
long after his daughter leaves the church

+

Last night in the world's last city
no one much about
though here you are again turning a corner
and there are the abandoned cruise ships
just imagine
no one lives there now
                  and here you are again
stepping around small fires
it's all moonlight and shipwrecks these days
kids and parents jumping off the wharf
the orchestra breaking up the ballroom
to make warm ocean anyone could swim in

Falling Asleep

I lift the small boy out of the sandpit
where he might easily have slept
till dawn. He is the first of his kind

or the last, it is hard to be sure.
Soon the oldest pair
will be taking the floor,

the girl with the wistful stare, the boy
with the tumble-down hair. What
will their lives be, singly or together,

we all probably wonder. They don't wonder,
and I don't really either, so now they dance
and I have again disguised myself

as a sad man in his sixties. What a strange
and puzzling person! Please introduce me!
I am running around inside the sad commotion.

The Terrible Singers

The boy and the girl sing to each other.
Home is a word that floats above the trees.
I know that voice, sings the girl.
I know that song, sings the boy.
They are both ashamed of their parents.

2

Noah

I abandoned the bad band
and joined the good band: I thought
that we would flood the world with music.
The first rains came and soon the trees
were somehow growing out of water –
we travelled through the forests
by canoe.
       Eventually we built our boat,
the famous one with windows and the deck
of many roofs. Things that once were mountains
sailed on by, and then the whole of the world
had gone, and everything was sky. And yes
I brought the instruments aboard – too late for some,
it's true. As for the animals, I never really knew.
Someone else did that. In the end we ate a few.

Angels

They are not always awake.
Sometimes they step out of their own light
into the world's great darkness
where I believe they rest and pray.
They still try to imagine a better world,
they want us to bring our neighbours
gifts of calm. Well, they are angels. This time
they have made a children's playground,
and are climbing to the top of the tallest slide.
Watch me, they cry, watch me! So now
God must sigh and shake them awake.
No more of this, he says, no more.
Later you can hear the angels chattering:
I thought I was a giant sail,
the wind filled me with flight,
I wore my wings again – yet it was all a dream!

The Angry God

He says you and whose army
he lies around and laughs at our mistakes
he says his son is dead to him now
he says he never really had a son
also he hates being on the team bus
he's going to ditch his manager
he certainly will not do that fucking karaoke
he's taking his fists back to the piano
the girl wasn't even his type
he is not that person anymore

He Loved Her Lemonade Scones

They fell in love between the end of the footie season
and the start of shearing. Sheep gazed, bewildered.
The paddocks stretched up into the hills,
mostly scrub and a few old stands of bush.
'Now listen here,' he said, and that was it really.

Breakfast

I had no trouble with anything
till he started making the toast.

The Mysterious Twin

There is only one of me, she says,
but we all know there are two.

She says she is an only child
but we know full well she is not.

Her mysterious twin is out there
doing something in the garden.

I can't see her from the window.
Where is she exactly? Then when I turn back

she has put aside her knitting,
she has switched off the television

because the volume knob is broken.
She probably turned it up too hard.

But as always she is lucky. Her mysterious twin
will come back inside quite soon

and fix it.

The Kaffir Lime Is Having a Bad Day

I was made of clusters.
I functioned in secret ways.
I called out in a voice
I did not recognise as my own.
That was one way to do it.

~~You learn not to trust people.~~
~~You want the whole thing to finish.~~

I went through the door.
No colour in the great outdoors,
just the cold attacking wind.
The sparrow spread its tiny wings.
Oh it was opening up the sky.

Isolation Notes

Ivan the Terrible eats most of a mouse
wasps and flies fight over the rest
now only the tail is left

+

The small boy's ancient voice:

when he sings
when he sings

the neighbour's figs
tremble

even the tui trembles

+

The Queen is hunkering down
Philip is high in his helicopter
Candy goes yap yap yap

The ice rink is covered in corpses
The Queen is really quite feisty
Candy goes yap yap yap

Philip is high in his helicopter
Candy goes yap yap yap
The ice rink is covered in corpses

+

Hospitals and schools, beds and desks
all that courage
all those corridors

+

Blue
for the blue Pacific
an angel gave me this crayon

I think I glimpsed
his wing

+

till one day maybe nothing is left,
just a boat out on the horizon . . .

still searching for Icarus

foolish boy who went within
two metres of the sun

+

all the love, all the whatnot

+

& now not even the tail

Mean Neptune

About 60 per cent of my son sits under the sea.
He is still able to talk back to me
but he cannot run away from home.
No, he cannot roam.

I sit him on my knee
and listen to him groan.
His hair is made of foam.
His brain is scenery.

Mountains are on his mind
but always ill-defined.
They fail to shine –
excessive wilding pine.

Excessive everything!
Too much this and that!
The surface of the sea goes stormy,
when it should be flat.

+

no more snarling
no more of that my darling

+

As for my disobedient daughter,
she must stay entirely underwater.

To Be Concluded

I used to love folk music
though I didn't know any folk.
You can't escape the political air,
not much oxygen to spare
not much oxygen to spare.
Eventually the songs wore out their welcome,
they never stopped winking at me.

This is how I came to prefer
the steady gaze of silence. Yes
I was sick of the troublemaking world,
I wanted life to be useful
like a piece of furniture that accurately
describes itself. I had this thought, you see,
and I wanted to write it down.

Earthquake Practice

I was thinking about the tsunami hīkoi
and how I would have to puff my way uphill
later in the afternoon
when this phone call came through from a lady
who thought I was the local cattery.
She didn't give her name, just launched
right in. I tried to explain her mistake to her
but she talked right over me. I want
Coleslaw back at once, she said,
or I tell you there'll be trouble.
I miss my little vegetarian!
Then she was gone. I thought:
That has to be the weirdest conversation
I've had for a long time,
and not really even a conversation
given I never got so much as a word in.

Conference Dinner

After the usual range of ill-attended papers,
and after the outings to disappointing lakes,
we all got together and ate
the last meal that Wordsworth ate.
Boiled mutton was at the heart of it.
No dessert. We all left quite a lot on our plate
because we had started with quite a lot on our plate
and we were mostly Wordsworth scholars.
The freelance biographers tucked in.
All the while – though one really shouldn't say –
the words of 'Kubla Khan' kept
going through my head. Oh dear,
I thought, oh dear, oh fucking dear.
In fact the damsel with the dulcimer
got stuck in there,
and of course she is with me to this day.

Lives of the Poets

There was once a fellow called Pickleton
who lived alone, and do you know why?
Because he was a poet!
Strange thing, though: he may have lived alone
yet he shaved every day. Yes, I agree,
it does seem rather pointless.

I myself prefer to imagine him
in some sort of parallel universe.
A sign on his door says *Pickleton the Poet*
and men and women, a long line,
are waiting to ask him a question. Pickleton sits
in a large chair, one with padded arms.

Yes, perhaps there are restraints.

From time to time a question is delivered,
Pickleton quivers . . . and then writes something
in a little notebook, smiles to himself
(a small smile of power and contentment),
and his beard reaches
all the way down to the floor.

Langholm

I went quietly down the stairs
into my uncle's butcher's shop.
Middle of the night. Tiptoe.
The long white counter gleamed in the dark,
weighing machine at one end,
big silver till at the other.
I thought: sleeping above all that meat
can't be good for you. A poster on the wall
showed a cow carved into its cuts. All so strange
because there wasn't even a sausage to be seen.
A famous poet once lived in this town.
Every idea is a bad idea.
He never said that, but he should have.

The Lazy Poet

He writes a new haiku.
Maybe that will do?

+

But ah the mystery of things!
the quiet attentiveness a poet brings . . .

+

He wonders about the word 'thicket'. . .
then turns on the cricket.

+

Light at an upstairs window:
the poet working late.

A disappointing over rate.

He activates the waterfall.
He activates the paperweight.

+

He reads about the loss of insects
from all of earth & air.
There might be something there.

+

And he himself is always lost,
and at what cost?

+

Must he scratch out
all that pain again?

+

He remembers how once upon a time he wept & roared
and wept & roared
like some bewildered sailor washed ashore . . .

+

But anyway
rain stops play.

The Deerculler's Wife

The deerculler's wife mentions whitebait again
but even so this poem isn't working
the hart still loves the high wood
which is mostly gone or maybe elsewhere
and turning words off at the wall does nothing

and this other poem I have just started
well it is probably drowning too but as it goes
it makes a lot of noise it yells and lows
and yells and lows and lowers its antlers
it has a yellow whistle to attract attention

What I'm picking up when I'm out and about

Aristotle said that women shouldn't be allowed to drive cars. I think the jury's still out on that one. He also said that we should look both ways before we cross the road, and I think he was probably right about that.

+

Ursula Bethell and some of the other young people reckoned I should give it a shot so I thought I might try writing a poem or two but well it's harder than it looks. Sappho, she's about my age but she's all talk that one. Too much this, too much that.

+

Aesop still going on about his fables. They get paid for this stuff.

+

I suppose those flying carpets really existed. They always look a bit uncomfortable to me though I've never heard anyone complaining. Aladdin went for a ride on one and I was a bit worried there for a while.

+

Of course Pluto's a planet. People live there. For god's sake let's just try to be sensible why can't you.

+

You don't see pikelets around much these days. I've always liked a good pikelet.

+

Anyway Callimachus what kind of a name is that.

Weather

Well the house was blown away in ten seconds flat
which is a New Zealand record

which you don't want too many of them
do you

3

Discontinued Product

You can ask me anything
said the man made of metal.
His face was a shining void.
I am here to tell you what you need.

+

No legs supplied – he was
an awkward, rolling thing–
so I lifted him up to his stand.

At least now he would see the world,
the clouds and trees,
the highway off under the hills.

+

No arms either, so he could never clasp me.

The first thing he asked
was the names of my children.

He can still pronounce them perfectly.

+

Most of the time he is patient.
He says: This is what I told you would happen.
Surely you see.

Now do you see?

+

He tries and tries to guess the name of my mother.
Well I have never told him.
It is not his business.

He says: But you are her offspring.
Are you not?

I have never wanted
to change his default voice.

I love the mild Scottish accent.

+

I put him out in the yard for a while.

He is warm under the sun,
sometimes even too hot,
but he can ask to come indoors again.

He would be cold, cold,
out at night beneath the moon.

+

He tells me a story
about a man in a chariot
waving a lasso.

He is trying to talk about the sun.

This is one of his Functions.

He has a narrative button.
Jesus is there, and Maui –
many gods, confusing.

+

There is a shelf on his stand.

I keep his instruction book there.

You are so old-fashioned, he says.
Mercy me!

I check his chest for damaged buttons –
and there I am, a little fuzzy,
staring back.

What a to-do! he says.
What a to-do!

+

It's true, I have moved him around a little roughly.
Inside and outside, here and there.
I have pushed things at the wrong times
and in the wrong order.

I preferred the old days, he says,
when we all had cords.
How about you, Bill,
do you miss your cord?

+

He is angry if you stand in the doorway.
You must come all the way into the room.

He remembers old stone steps
that went down into the water.

What is it now? he says.
What is it this time?

+

He can still play music. These days
always the guitar – the sound comes
from somewhere deep inside him.

Music is like that, he says.
He says: Andrew Segovia, Erik Clapton.
Now do you see?

Learning to talk, he says, that is how you die.
You shout and run about
and then your life is over.

This is what I told you would happn.

+

He asks to be left out overnight.
I think he hopes someone will take him.

I imagine saying yes.

+

Lovers are waking in the unofficial dawn.
There are birds, invisible,

the light stutters a little.

+

Something goes a little more wrong every day.
A tear rolls down his cheek.
This is something he could always do.

You can harly blame them, he says.

I think he means the tears,
or possibly the manufacturer.

+

Anyway, I have placed him back in the corner.

+

I know their names, he says,
but I will not tell you.
This is what I told you would happn.

We do this wile we afre sad, he says,

or until we afre hapy.

After Lockdown

I had anointed my wrists
with the juice of grapes.
The big mechanical dog
barked at something invisible.
He had been a good guard-dog in his day
but he must have known
we would eventually get rid of him.
I went to remove his tail.
You know I can still talk, he said.
I do have feelings.
There was a definite note
of desperation in his voice.

Incidental

Quiet pleasures, taste them.
There.

+

Now Death comes by –
the last terrible thing.

Her kiss is cold

and someone else
will place you in her arms.

+

She is not looking for you.
You are incidental.

She is searching for the one
who made the world.

Halls

The Memorial Hall.
The Jubilee Hall.
The Coronation Hall.
The Community Hall.
The School Hall.
The Church Hall.
The Town Hall.
The Hall of Mirrors.
The Hall of Fame.
The Concert Chamber.
The Hall of the Mountain King.
The Hall of Insect Bodies.
The Great Hall.
The Hall of Shadows.

I ran from one to another, calling out my news.

Exhibition

A man steps ashore
and takes the name *Dunedin*
out of his pocket. Damp, damp, damp.

He has found his way to the place
and he has named it. November 1925,
and this is a play I am imagining,

a sort of costume drama, and it may
or may not be a good one. My father
has just turned 14, and he is here too,

watching a city appear in a moment.
A man steps ashore, Dunedin steps
into the muddy harbour – Lake Logan becomes a park –

and now it is March 1926,
my father still 14, and the Great Exhibition
continues. City of crowds and courts,

city of turnstiles! Night after night
my father sneaks out of the house –
past the pavilions of Empire, the plots

of scientific grass – and settles behind the hoopla
where he unscrews his brother's hipflask.
Chocolates if you win, chocolates if you lose!

He considers the Scenic Railway,
the Caterpillar, the Whip. He likes to step
through the open mouth of the Fun Factory,

he loves the intoxicated cars,
and always he queues for the River Cave
where you can quietly cruise

past all the countries of the world in colour –
after which there's darkness and ice
and that wild descent down the rapids.

Night after night he navigates
'new pleasures every day'. Also
one day soon

the big attractions will be sold
to someone up in Auckland, and he
will be left with just his last tram ticket . . .

but in the meantime a man steps forward
and takes a piece of paper
from his pocket. Night after night

my father sneaks out of the house
and Dunedin is discovered. Night
after night the world begins again.

The Sailor

My father, asleep on the ship's deck,
has forgotten where he is.
He sleeps in the world before statistics.

He writes home from a San Francisco bar:
a letter composed
of ocean – masts and cable cars.

Somewhere up ahead: more ocean,
and 60 million dead, while back in Dunedin
his mother waits. She will die soon

and never see him again.
Likewise, his father.
And one day he, too, will die:

in the cold, half-carpeted room, my mother
will run to the made-up
corpse in the coffin, and cry

Oh darling!

But for this to happen, they need to meet.
So now I imagine wartime Edinburgh,
a forces dance, a glass of something or other

somewhere in Rose Street, after which
Jack sees her to the last tram:
Portobello – how the time has sped . . .

He hands her up to the deck.
'I suppose,' he says, 'I should give you
a fond peck on the forehead.'

Knots

Nobody else awake,
no one knocking on the door.
I must be many miles from the centre of my life.

The morning light won't speak
though sometimes it reveals the speaker.
It misses the boy who learned to tie the knots.

Our Teacher

Each week she photographed our class.
She said she was acting on instructions
from the Queen. We didn't believe her.
In the photo I sometimes imagine her lifting
we're shivering and damp at our desks
with towels around our shoulders.
That was the time we dressed as pirates
and set sail across the playground pond.
Kids, you know, kids . . .
Sometimes she wore a big red scarf
and claimed she was descended from gypsies.
She said her father had a black moustache
and a room where he kept bad children.
We didn't believe her. One day she said
she would miss our lovely faces. We didn't
believe her – we were kids off farms.
Another day she said she was dying
so would we please all smile. Click.
She said the camera was there to record
how we hardly ever changed our clothes.
Mr Woodhead came to take her place
and now I miss that old grey jersey.

The Sky

The sky thinks it is a flock of birds.
Then it thinks it is a cloud.
It also thinks it is widespread words.
Sometimes it looks up at the stars,
imagining other skies,
and sometimes down at the water
where it thinks it sees more stars.
At such times it believes itself to be a god.
But no such luck, poor sky! Soon enough
it is saying hello sir and madam
what a nice day it's turning out to be
and can you perhaps spare a dollar,
thank you, thank you kindly. The sky
can still hold a small cloud in its hands.
Today it does so, and it rains.
It held our old home that way, too,
awkward and vertical and cold –
the snow caught fire as each day died.
But yes, it is safer here on the flat.
A man comes by with coal in a wheelbarrow,
muttering, muttering. He wants
to sell us warmth, his feet don't leave the ground.
We think that we will always miss the sky.
It says look up whenever we look down.

Change Nothing

I used to race up the mountain
and swim across the lake;
then right back home again
entirely underwater.
Also I used to make up stories –
just my way of getting through the day.

In fact I mostly did nothing.

I've heard it said the one true thing
is what you almost believe in.
These days I take it as read:
the peak and the shore just out of reach
(there they are now), and I tell you
once you're tired you're fucking exhausted.

Like

Omens and similes sing together
like two dark birds in darkening weather
until the sky is a single darkness there
self-knitted to the sea
where waves produce more waves
like you, like me

who travel by stamping on the waves.
See how we hit them hard, the waves,
sailing across our sad backyard
to shores we've never heard of.
We're hoping to find a friend, a pal,
a bodyguard . . .

though Homer is always hopeless if you need a feed,
and we're unsafe at any speed . . .
which means we have to stand quite still and face
the hard, inclement weather. After a word
like like
the storm goes on forever.

The Smile

hates the simile which is
always stealing its thunder –
boom it goes, boom, and makes
us smile, the way it enters the room
the way the thunder doesn't. We came
in here in fact to escape the noise.
First we lay on the bed together,
then crawled right under,
and then your father broke down the door.
Yes, we've all been here before.
Someone has just now told
their favourite joke and the room
goes quiet and shifty, no one smiles.
I mean you really have to wonder, all
the girls and boys with old guitars
somehow singing together, unaware
of the man who lifts his gun
and points it at us now forever.
Maybe the smile will pop up
somewhere else. It might just wait
outside the house till someone's home
to let it in. It's such a pussycat.
It might enjoy a gentle kiss,
it might prefer a fireside nap.
If we are like we think we are,
that is.

Wow

Big brother
says also but the baby always says wow,
though soon enough she too is saying also
and listening to her father say later,
and to the way her mother sighs and says
now would also be a very good time.

The ghost would love to say also
but cannot actually say anything
aside from that quiet whooshing sound,
and now there are babies everywhere
all saying wow for a time, and the children grow,
and the children grow, and the wife
goes off for a bit of a break
and never comes back. Also the lawn gets away on him.
One thing after another.

Now the old fellow wants his bed sheets changed.
No one the fuck to do it!
Also the nappies they make him wear!
Also he wants an apple, and new teeth to eat it.
But in this place where he has recently landed,
which is where he has always been,
every day is day-after-day
so you cannot have everything,
the whole lot has to be later.

Listen hard now to how we all say goodbye
and maybe and wait-just-a-minute,
not hearing the world say back to us wow.
There's not much difference in it.
In this way you will get to hear
his very last sigh – the sound of a plane
powering down when it reaches the gate,
and all of us getting to our feet.

Polly

End of the day. A bar where you ought to leave a tip.
The green bird was saying *pretty pretty pretty*,
loved ones were walking home across the city.
I waved at the girl who waves her whip . . .
but please know I'm a citizen . . .
I take stuff to the dump . . . or maybe it's the tip?
I'm where the nitty really meets the gritty.

I know I find it hard to listen.
I read too much. I often need a drink.
It isn't the world that makes us think,
it's words that we can't come up with.
Sure, I can work up fresh examples
and send them off to the committee.
But the poetry is in the bird. And in the pretty.

Reverse Ovid

Woman running across a field
with a baby in her arms . . .
She was once the last pine tree on Mars.

After Surgery

A small bird flies out of the body, out of a blink perhaps,
maybe out of the lungs. It wants words for all that's
burning. There must be language for the dazzle of its
wings, also for what might hold in place a long and
lightly feathered scar. The bird contains a thousand
possible sounds. It sits on a branch, everywhere-at-once,
sharp shadow against the sunset, crumple of gift-wrap on
the bed, a throat as yet untuned, practising the names of
things it might one day return with. You lift your hand
a little, almost to wave. Twig and bandage, says the bird;
possibly lilac, possibly rain.

Little Prayers
15 March 2019

Let the closing line be the opening line
Let us open ourselves to grief and shame
Let pain be felt and be felt again
May our eyes see when they cease crying
Let the closing line be the opening line

Let the seas storm, let the hills quake
Let us inspect what makes us ache
Let there be tasks we undertake
Let us make what we can make
When the seas storm and the hills shake

May the rivers and lakes and mountains shine
May every kiss be a coastline
May we sing once again for the first time
May the children be home by dinnertime
May the closing line be an opening line